TABLE OF CONTENTS

Table of Contents 1

Introduction 2

Chapter 1: Overview of the SAEE 3

Chapter 2: Preparing for the SAEE 4

    Logic-Based Reasoning 5

    Experience Inventory, Part 1 21

    Language Usage 22

    Experience Inventory, Part 2 34

    Detail Observation 35

Chapter 3: SAEE Test Preparation 49

INTRODUCTION

The purpose of this preparation guide is to help you prepare to take the Special Agent Entrance Exam (SAEE). This guide will familiarize you with the sections of the SAEE and provide you with sample test questions and explanations for the correct answers to these questions.

The preparation guide is organized into three chapters. The first chapter provides an introduction to the test, to include summary information about the five sections of the test. The second chapter provides detailed instructions of each test section and sample test questions with explanations. The final chapter provides information on test preparation including test taking tips.

Please note: As you complete the SAEE, please describe yourself and your experiences honestly and accurately. Responses on this test are subject to verification by others. Cheating, deliberate attempts to falsify information or other dishonest conduct when completing the test may lead to your disqualification from the application process and from seeking Federal employment in the future. If you are a current Federal employee, you may be removed or debarred from Federal Service (5 C.F.R. part 731).

CHAPTER 1: OVERVIEW OF THE SAEE

The SAEE was developed to assess the range of skills and abilities required for successful performance in the Special Agent position. It is a paper-and-pencil exam, consisting of multiple-choice questions. The SAEE is made up of five separately timed sections:

Section 1: Logic-Based Reasoning. This section contains 12 passages, each of which describes a set of facts. Each passage is followed by 1 to 4 test questions that are conclusions based on the set of facts presented in the passage. Applicants read the passage and then decide whether each conclusion is true, false, or there is insufficient information to decide. Section 1 contains 30 questions. Applicants will have 40 minutes to complete this section.

Section 2: Experience Inventory, Part 1. This section contains statements that describe situations that applicants may or may not have encountered before. They must choose the response option that best describes the frequency with which they have been involved in the situation. Section 2 contains 64 questions. Applicants will have 20 minutes to complete this section.

Section 3: Language Usage. This section contains 2 types of documents (i.e., memoranda and summary reports). Errors have been incorporated into these documents and applicants are asked to identify errors in grammar, syntax, punctuation, usage, and/or structure. Section 3 contains 25 questions. Applicants will have 40 minutes to complete this section.

Section 4: Experience Inventory, Part 2. This section contains statements that describe different situations and opinions. Applicants must choose the response option that best reflects the extent to which their past supervisors and/or teachers would agree that the statement describes them. Section 4 contains 96 questions. Applicants will have 30 minutes to complete this section.

Section 5: Detail Observation. In this section, applicants are presented with a series of photographs. These photographs depict images that may be seen when working in the Special Agent job. For example, a photograph may depict a rope line or a city street during a surveillance operation. After viewing the photographs, applicants answer a series of questions unrelated to the photographs. Then, applicants answer a series of questions about what appeared in the photographs, but they are not permitted to view the photographs while answering these questions. This section contains 3 photographs and 3 sets of accompanying questions and takes approximately 40 minutes to complete.

CHAPTER 2: PREPARING FOR THE SAEE

GENERAL INSTRUCTIONS

The following are general instructions for taking the SAEE:

- Testing will begin **on time**. Applicants who arrive late will <u>not</u> be admitted.

- You will need to bring a photo ID to the testing site. Acceptable forms of photo ID include a valid driver's license, U.S. Passport, state-issued identification card, or U.S. military ID card.

- You will not be allowed to have any personal belongings (i.e., bags, newspapers, etc.) at your testing station.

- All cell phones and other electronic devices must be turned off during testing.

- The test administrator will time all test sections. However, ample time has been allotted for you to complete each section. For sections lasting 20 minutes or longer, you will be told when you have 5 minutes remaining.

- Once you have completed the questions in a test section, you will need to wait for instructions before moving on to the next section.

- Do not spend too much time on any one question. If you finish a test section early, you will be able to check your answers to the questions *in that section only*. You may not work ahead or return to a previous section.

- If you leave a response to a question blank, it will be scored the same as an incorrect answer. If you are unsure of an answer, you should choose the option that is your best guess.

- Applicants will not be permitted to leave the testing room. If you need to use the restroom, you must raise your hand and turn in your test materials to the test administrator before leaving. You will not be afforded any extra time for the test. In this situation, applicants will only be allowed to leave the room one at a time.

- If you have any questions concerning the instructions or the test, please ask a test administrator. Do not discuss the test content, including your answers, with other test takers.

- You will be notified of testing results by e-mail, within five to ten business days of taking the test.

LOGIC-BASED REASONING

OVERVIEW

This section contains 12 passages, each of which describes a set of facts. Each passage is followed by 1 to 4 test questions that are conclusions based on the set of facts presented in the passage. You will read the passage and then decide whether each conclusion is true, false, or there is insufficient information to decide. **This section contains 30 questions and you will have 40 minutes to complete it.** Ample time has been provided for this test section. Do not spend too much time on any one question; if you finish early, you may go back and review your responses within this section.

Logic-based reasoning is involved in a variety of job-related situations that require critical thinking, problem solving, judgment, and decision-making. The questions in this section of the SAEE will assess your ability to comprehend information that is presented and draw conclusions from that information. This will require you to read carefully and think about the information that is provided as well as the information that is not provided.

Reasoning involves drawing conclusions based on the information that is available. Conclusions are valid when they are justified given the evidence. Reasoning allows an individual to understand which conclusions can and cannot be drawn based on statements provided. Sometimes conclusions are not necessarily true or false because complete information is not available.

Further explanation for how to approach logic-based reasoning questions is provided next.

TYPES OF STATEMENTS

There are a number of different types of statements that are used in the passages and questions for the Logic-based Reasoning Test. The types of statements and examples in this section describe how you should use information provided about groups or categories in the test.

"All" Statements

A statement about two groups often begins with the word "all" or "every." These statements tell you that everything in the first group is also in the second group. However, the statement does not allow you to conclude that everything in the second group is also in the first group.

Example Statement: All Secret Service Special Agents are U.S. government employees.
Invalid conclusion: All government employees are Secret Service Special Agents.
Valid conclusion: Some U.S. government employees are Secret Service Special Agents.

"No" statements

These statements indicate that one group is not part of another group. These statements may use the words "none" or "not" and allow you to conclude that these two groups have no common members. You can conclude that the members of either group are not members of the other group.

Example Statement: No U.S. Senators are under 30 years of age.
Invalid conclusion: Some people under 30 years of age are U.S. Senators.
Valid conclusion: No one under 30 years of age is a U.S. Senator.

"Some" statements

These statements refer to part of a group by using terms such as "some," "most," "a few," or another term which indicates a portion of a group. Such statements about a portion of a group imply nothing about the remaining portion of the group. You should not jump to a conclusion that you might make in typical conversational speech.

Example Statement: Many Secret Service Special Agents are not from Alaska.
Invalid conclusion: A few Secret Service Special Agents are from Alaska.
Valid conclusion: A few Secret Service Special Agents may or may not be from Alaska.

"If-then" statements

These statements provide information about a sequence of events that will happen or has already happened. These statements may also use terms such as "whenever" or "every time." Such statements let you know that the events must follow the specified order and may not be reversed. Additionally, the events may not be negated <u>and</u> follow the same order. To validly reverse the order, the statements must be negated.

Example Statement: If a person is charged with identity theft, then the person will be put on trial.
Invalid conclusion: If a person is put on trial, then the person has been charged with identity theft.
Invalid conclusion: If a person is not charged with identity theft, then the person will not be put on trial.
Valid conclusion: If a person has not been put on trial, then the person has not been charged with identity theft.

TEST DIRECTIONS

The Logic Based Reasoning section consists of 12 passages, each of which describes a set of facts. Each passage is followed by 1 to 4 test questions that are conclusions based on the set of facts presented in the passage. Read the passage and then decide whether each conclusion is:

> **True**, which means that you can infer the conclusion from the facts given; or
>
> **False**, which means that the conclusion is contrary to the facts given; or whether there is
>
> **Insufficient information to decide**, which means that there is insufficient information for you to determine whether the facts imply the conclusion or are contrary to the conclusion.

You must use *only* the information provided in the passage, without using any outside information.

Some of the passages include terms that describe the likelihood that something will occur. For example, "it is more likely than not that I will be in the office today." For the purposes of this test, likelihood statements are defined as follows:

> **Definitely:** 100% likely to happen
> **More likely than not:** more than 50% likely to happen
> **Less likely than not:** less than 50% likely to happen

Use the following response option guide to mark your answer sheet:

a) **True**
b) **False**
c) **Insufficient Information to Decide**

Note: You will only be using response options A, B, or C on your answer sheet for this section. Please be careful not to mark the other response options provided.

PREPARATION TIPS

1. Thoroughly read through the descriptions of the types of statements above; be sure you understand what is meant by "all," "some," and "no" within the context of this test.

2. Remember that the words described above are used more precisely in the Logic-based Reasoning section compared to everyday usage. Read the section above on how everyday language is more precisely used in this test.

3. Do NOT use any outside information to reach your conclusions. You should ONLY use the information provided in the test., even if the topic of the question is something you have additional information about,

4. Read through the passages very carefully and be attentive to words that may affect how you answer the question. For example, words like "not" or "all" likely have an impact on the answer to questions about the passage.

5. Review each of the sample questions on the following pages. Read the explanation for each question to ensure that you understand why the conclusion was drawn.

LOGIC BASED REASONING SAMPLE QUESTIONS

Passage 1:

Melinda is a Secret Service Special Agent.
Susan has never been to Georgia.
All Secret Service Special Agents have been to Georgia.
Fred works with Susan.

Indicate whether the statement is True, False, or if there is Insufficient Information to draw a conclusion.

1. Susan is a Secret Service Special Agent.
    a) True
    b) False
    c) Insufficient Information to Decide

2. Fred works for the Secret Service.
    a) True
    b) False
    c) Insufficient Information to Decide

3. Melinda has been to Georgia.
    a) True
    b) False
    c) Insufficient Information to Decide

Passage 1 Explanations:

1. The first conclusion is **FALSE**. The facts state that Susan has never been to Georgia and that all Secret Service Special Agents have been to Georgia. Therefore, Susan cannot be a Secret Service Special Agent. You would fill in the bubble that corresponds to "B" on your answer sheet for **FALSE**.

2. You cannot tell from the facts presented whether the second conclusion is true or false. We know that Susan cannot be a Secret Service Special Agent, because she has not been to Georgia and all Secret Service Special Agents have been to Georgia. But she may work at the Secret Service in a different job, or she may work for another employer. This means that Fred, who works with Susan, also may or may not work for the Secret Service. You would fill in the bubble that corresponds to "C" on your answer sheet for **INSUFFICIENT INFORMATION TO DECIDE**.

3. The third conclusion is **TRUE**. The facts state that Melinda is a Secret Service Special Agent and that all Secret Service Special Agents have been to Georgia. Therefore, Melinda has been to Georgia. You would fill in the bubble that corresponds to "A" on your answer sheet for **TRUE**.

Passage 2:

Mark completed more investigations than Jake.
Megan completed fewer investigations than Mark.
Jake completed more investigations than Rob.

Indicate whether the statement is True, False, or if there is Insufficient Information to draw a conclusion.

1. Jake completed more investigations than Megan.
   a) True
   b) False
   c) Insufficient Information to Decide

2. Mark completed more investigations than Rob.
   a) True
   b) False
   c) Insufficient Information to Decide

3. Mark completed fewer investigations than Rob.
   a) True
   b) False
   c) Insufficient Information to Decide

Passage 2 Explanations:

1. We only know that Mark completed more investigations than both Jake and Megan, but we don't know whether Jake or Megan completed more investigations compared to each other. You would fill in the bubble that corresponds to "C" on your answer sheet for ***INSUFFICIENT INFORMATION TO DECIDE***.

2. If Jake completed more investigations than Rob, and Mark completed more investigations than Jake, then we know that Mark completed more investigations than Rob. You would fill in the bubble that corresponds to "A" on your answer sheet for ***TRUE***.

3. Mark completed more investigations than Jake, Megan, and Rob. You would fill in the bubble that corresponds to "B" on your answer sheet for ***FALSE***.

Passage 3:

All task force agents work from either Boston or Chicago.

Some Boston task force agents are financial fraud investigators.

All Chicago task force agents are financial fraud investigators.

All Boston task force agents who are financial fraud investigators received financial investigation training.

No Chicago task force agents received financial investigation training.

All Chicago task force agents received cyber security training.

Indicate whether the statement is True, False, or if there is Insufficient Information to draw a conclusion.

1. No task force agents who received cyber security training are financial fraud investigators.
   a) True
   b) False
   c) Insufficient Information to Decide

2. No task force agents who received financial investigation training work from Chicago.
   a) True
   b) False
   c) Insufficient Information to Decide

3. No task force agents who received cyber security training work from Boston.
   a) True
   b) False
   c) Insufficient Information to Decide

Passage 3 Explanations:

1. We know that all Chicago task force agents received cyber security training, and we also know that all Chicago task force agents are financial fraud investigators. Therefore, this statement cannot be true. You would fill in the bubble that corresponds to "B" on your answer sheet for **FALSE**.

2. Chicago task force agents did not receive financial investigation training. Therefore, this statement must be true. You would fill in the bubble that corresponds to "A" on your answer sheet for **TRUE**.

3. We know that Chicago task force agents received cyber security training. We do not have information about cyber security training for Boston task force agents. Therefore, you would fill in the bubble that corresponds to "C" on your answer sheet for **INSUFFICIENT INFORMATION TO DECIDE**.

Passage 4:

All Secret Service Special Agents hired in the last 5 years received information technology training.
Only Secret Service Special Agents can receive the information technology training.
Some Secret Service Special Agents have not received the information technology training.
Julie was hired last year as a Secret Service Special Agent.
Allen has received the information technology training.

Indicate whether the statement is True, False, or if there is Insufficient Information to draw a conclusion.

1. Allen was hired as a Secret Service Special Agent within the last 5 years.
    a) True
    b) False
    c) Insufficient Information to Decide

2. Allen is a Secret Service Special Agent.
    a) True
    b) False
    c) Insufficient Information to Decide

3. Julie has not received information technology training.
    a) True
    b) False
    c) Insufficient Information to Decide

Passage 4 Explanations:

1. You cannot tell from the facts presented whether the first conclusion is true or false. According to the statements, all Secret Service Special Agents hired within the last 5 years have received information technology training and some Secret Service Special Agents have not received the training. However, we do not know whether or not Secret Service Special Agents hired more than 5 years ago have received the training. You would fill in the bubble that corresponds to "C" on your answer sheet for ***INSUFFICIENT INFORMATION TO DECIDE.***

2. The second conclusion is ***TRUE***. The facts state that only Secret Service Special Agents can receive the information technology training and that Allen has received the information technology training. Therefore, Allen must be a Secret Service Special Agent. You would fill in the bubble that corresponds to "A" on your answer sheet for ***TRUE***.

3. The third conclusion is ***FALSE***. The facts state that all Secret Service Special Agents hired within the last 5 years have received the information technology training and that Julie was hired last year as a Secret Service Special Agent. Therefore, Julie must have received the training. You would fill in the bubble that corresponds to "B" on your answer sheet for ***FALSE***.

Passage 5:

Jim and Amy work in the same office.
Eric and Amy both have the same position within the Secret Service.
Amy is a Secret Service Special Agent.
Jim and Eric are working on the same assignment.
There are only 2 Secret Service Special Agents at Jim and Amy's office.

Indicate whether the statement is True, False, or if there is Insufficient Information to draw a conclusion.

1. Eric is a Secret Service Special Agent.
    a) True
    b) False
    c) Insufficient Information to Decide

2. Jim is not a Secret Service Special Agent.
    a) True
    b) False
    c) Insufficient Information to Decide

3. Eric and Jim are both Secret Service Special Agents and work at the same office.
    a) True
    b) False
    c) Insufficient Information to Decide

Passage 5 Explanations:

1. The first conclusion is **TRUE**. The facts state that Amy is a Secret Service Special Agent and that both Eric and Amy hold the same position. Therefore, Eric must be a Secret Service Special Agent. You would fill in the bubble that corresponds to "A" on your answer sheet for **TRUE**.

2. You cannot tell from the facts presented whether the second conclusion is true or false. The facts state that Amy is a Secret Service Special Agent, who holds the same position as Eric. We know that Jim and Eric are working on the same assignment. The facts also state that Jim and Amy work in the same office but that there are only two Secret Service Special Agents in that office. However, because we do not know which office Eric works from, we cannot be sure that Jim is not also a Secret Service Special Agent. You would fill in the bubble that corresponds to "C" on your answer sheet for **INSUFFICIENT INFORMATION TO DECIDE**.

3. The third conclusion is **FALSE**. The facts state that both Eric and Amy are Secret Service Special Agents and that Jim and Amy work in the same office. We also know that there are only two Secret Service Special Agents at Jim and Amy's office. Therefore, Jim and Eric could not both be Secret Service Special Agents at the same office, because we know that Amy is a Secret Service Special Agent at Jim's office. You would fill in the bubble that corresponds to "B" on your answer sheet for **FALSE**.

Passage 6:

No part-time employees are Secret Service Special Agents.
All part-time employees report to a field office location.
Some full-time employees are Secret Service Special Agents.
Christopher reports to the Maryland field office.
Brian is a Secret Service Special Agent.

Indicate whether the statement is True, False, or if there is Insufficient Information to draw a conclusion.

1. Christopher is a part-time employee.
    a) True
    b) False
    c) Insufficient Information to Decide

2. Brian is a full-time employee.
    a) True
    b) False
    c) Insufficient Information to Decide

3. All full-time Secret Service employees are Special Agents.
    a) True
    b) False
    c) Insufficient Information to Decide

Passage 6 Explanations:

1. You cannot tell from the facts presented whether the first conclusion is true or false. The facts state that all part-time employees report to a field office location and that Christopher reports to the Maryland field office location. However, the facts do not indicate that only part-time employees report to the Maryland field office or that no full-time employees report to field office locations. Therefore, it cannot be assumed that Christopher is a part-time employee from the facts presented. You would fill in the bubble that corresponds to "C" on your answer sheet for **INSUFFICIENT INFORMATION TO DECIDE**.

2. The second conclusion is **TRUE**. We know that all Secret Service Special Agents are full-time employees. Brian is a Secret Service Special Agent. Therefore, Brian must be a full-time employee. You would fill in the bubble that corresponds to "A" on your answer sheet for **TRUE**.

3. The third conclusion is **FALSE**. We know that all Secret Service Special Agents are full-time employees. We also know that some full-time Secret Service employees are Special Agents. Therefore, some Secret Service full-time employees must hold titles other than Special Agent. You would fill in the bubble that corresponds to "B" on your answer sheet for **FALSE**.

EXPERIENCE INVENTORY, PART 1

OVERVIEW

The Experience Inventory is administered in 2 parts. Part 1 contains statements that describe situations that you may or may not have encountered before.

For example, you may see questions such as:

1. Maintained a to-do list to organize your work.//
2. Had a difficult time getting your point across.
3. Worked on a task to help the team even though it was not a required part of your job.

You will choose the response option that best describes the frequency with which you have been involved in the situation (see below for these options). This section of the test is only asking about your past experiences, so there is no way to study for these questions. Therefore, be as accurate as possible in your answer choices. **Section 2 contains 64 questions and you will have 20 minutes to complete this section.**

TEST DIRECTIONS

This section contains statements that describe situations that you may or may not have encountered before. Read each statement carefully and choose the response option that best describes the frequency with which you have been involved in the situation. If you have not been involved in the situation, choose the "Never" response option.

Use the following response option guide to respond to these statements:

> The frequency with which you have been involved in the situation is:
>
> a) Never
> b) Once or Twice
> c) Several Times
> d) Frequently or Routinely

Please respond as accurately and honestly as possible (some questions are designed to detect inaccurate self-descriptions). It is best to work at a fairly rapid pace, without spending too much time thinking about any one question or statement.

LANGUAGE USAGE

OVERVIEW

This section of the test assesses your language skills. It contains 2 types of documents (i.e., memoranda and summary reports). Errors have been inserted into these documents and you are asked to identify these errors in grammar, syntax, punctuation, usage, and/or structure. **This section contains 25 questions and you will have 40 minutes to complete this section.**

The following are definitions for the different types of errors that may occur in the Language Usage section:

Spelling

Spelling errors are words that are spelled incorrectly

Example. Spelling the word "investigation" incorrectly as "investigasion"

Subject-verb agreement

Subject-verb agreement is the grammatical rule that states that the verb must agree in number with its subject. An error occurs when a plural verb is used with a singular subject or a singular verb is used with a plural subject.

Example. Using "is" when the subject of the sentence is plural such as in this sentence: "The boys is going to the baseball game."

Punctuation

Errors in punctuation include errors in the use of periods, apostrophes, semi-colons, colons, and other types of punctuation.

Example. Improperly using "it's" as a possessive and not a contraction as in this sentence: "The dog hurt it's foot."

Capitalization

Errors in capitalization include capitalizing words that should not be capitalized and not capitalizing words that should be capitalized.

Example. "She wanted a new Flower for her window."

Formation of plurals

Errors in formation of plurals are a specific type of spelling error, which include when the plural form of a word is incorrect

Example. "Children" is the correct way to indicate more than one child, so writing "childs" is an incorrect use of plural formation.

Word usage

> An *improperly used word* is defined as correctly spelled, but inappropriately used in the sentence.
>
> **Example.** If a sentence refers to Austin as the "capitol" of Texas, this is an improperly used word because "capitol" refers to a building, not the "capital" of a state.

TEST DIRECTIONS

This section consists of two types of documents (i.e., memoranda and summary reports), each of which contains up to sixteen sentences. For each document, be sure to carefully read through the document and then respond to a number of multiple-choice questions. You should select the best answer from among the alternatives provided. Each question is independent of all other questions in the section. Therefore, you should not base your answer to one question on information presented in another question, unless otherwise instructed.

Errors have been purposefully inserted into the documents. As such, questions will refer to specific sentences in the document and will require that you identify any potential errors. Errors may include mistakes in one or more of the following forms: sentence structure, subject-verb agreement, punctuation, capitalization, spelling, the formation of plurals, or word use.

Because many experts disagree on the appropriate use of commas in a sentence, we are **not** testing for this type of error. Therefore, even if you believe that a comma should be present or omitted, **do not** count that as an error.

LANGUAGE USAGE SAMPLE QUESTIONS

Passage 1:

INTERAGENCY MEMORANDUM

Department of Homeland Security

United States Secret Service

TO: ALL EMPLOYEES
FROM: AMELIA GREGORY

SUBJECT: MILLIONS IN COUNTERFEIT U.S. CURRENCY RECOVERED

(1)On February 9, 2009, the Secret Service and the French National Police seized more than $60 millions in counterfeit U.S. bills. (2)The fake currency was found at an abandoned warehouse located in the heart of Paris, France. (3)A Secret Service representative, Chris Torrington, described the moment by saying, "This was one of the most substantial recovery I have encountered in my career. (4)I'm proud that were all able to witness such a major accomplishment." (5)According to french investigators, the operation in Paris was in the process of completing an order for $30 million in phony bills of various denominations. (6)Very little counterfeit operations have been able to fabricate such a large quantities of bogus notes. (7)Since 1999, the Secret Service has worked in partnership with local police authoritys in both France and Italy to fight a handful of counterfeit operations that has recently formed in these two countries. (8)In fact, regional offices in Paris and Rome were created in 2001. (9)As a result of joint efforts about the U.S. and national affiliates, more than $300 million in false currency have now been recovered. (10)Despite this success, the frequency of counterfeit crimes continue to escalate through out the world. (11)The Secret Service will continue to institute new partnerships with international authorities in its fight to defend the nation's financial infrastructure. (12)By 2020, the Secret Service plans to launch three new fully operational regional offices in capitol cities including Tokyo, Canberra, and Cairo. (13)The continued support of all Secret Service personnel is essential as we move forward in this endeavor.

Sincerely,
Amelia Gregory

Passage 1 Questions:

1. Which of the following sentences contains no errors?
   a) Sentence 3
   b) Sentence 4
   c) Sentence 10
   d) None of the Above

2. Which of the following sentences contains exactly two errors?
   a) Sentence 5
   b) Sentence 6
   c) Sentence 9
   d) Both B and C

3. Which of the following sentences contains an improperly used word?
   a) Sentence 2
   b) Sentence 8
   c) Sentence 11
   d) Sentence 12

4. Which of the following sentences contains both an error in subject-verb agreement AND a spelling error?
   a) Sentence 1
   b) Sentence 7
   c) Sentence 13
   d) None of the Above

5. Where is the most appropriate place to break the text into separate paragraphs?
   a) After sentence 4
   b) After sentence 5
   c) After sentence 6
   d) After sentence 7

6. Which of the following sentences, if deleted, would be least detrimental to the clarity of the memo?
   a) Sentence 1
   b) Sentence 7
   c) Sentence 9
   d) Sentence 10

7. Which of the following sentences contains an error in capitalization?
    a) Sentence 2
    b) Sentence 5
    c) Sentence 9
    d) Sentence 10

8. Which of the following sentences contains an error in subject-verb agreement?
    a) Sentence 1
    b) Sentence 10
    c) Sentence 12
    d) Sentence 13

Passage 1 Explanations:

1. Sentence 3 contains one error as "recovery" should be "recoveries." Sentence 4 contains one error as "were" is missing an apostrophe (e.g., it should be "we're"). Sentence 10 contains two errors as "continue" should be "continues" (this is an error in subject-verb agreement) and "through out" should be "throughout" (this is a spelling error). Thus, the correct response option is "**D**" as all of the sentences listed contain errors.

2. Sentence 5 contains no errors. Sentence 6 contains two errors as "little" should be "few" and "quantities" should be "quantity." Sentence 9 contains two errors as "about" should be "between" and "have" should be "has" (this is an error in subject-verb agreement). Thus, the correct response option is "**D**" as both Sentences 6 and 9 contain exactly two errors each.

3. Sentence 2 contains no errors. Sentence 8 contains no errors. Sentence 11 contains no errors. Sentence 12 contains one error as "capitol" should be "capital." This is considered an improperly used word because "capitol" should be "capital." This is an improperly used word and is NOT considered a spelling error because, though "capitol" is a real word and is correctly spelled, it has a different meaning than the appropriate word "capital." Thus, the correct response option is "**D**" because Sentence 12 contains an improperly used word.

4. Sentence 1 contains one error as "millions" should be "million." Sentence 7 contains two errors as "authoritys" should be "authorities" (this is a spelling error) and "has" should be "have" (this is an error in subject-verb agreement). Sentence 13 contains no errors. Thus, the correct response option is "**B**" because Sentence 7 contains an error in subject-verb agreement and a spelling error.

5. Sentences 5 and 6 continue to discuss the counterfeit currency recovered in France, along with the rest of the first paragraph. Therefore, they should both be included in the first paragraph. Sentence 7 begins a new section about previous partnership efforts and should therefore begin a new paragraph. Sentence 8 continues the section, following sentence 7 with "in fact," so it should remain in the same paragraph as sentence 7. Thus, the correct answer is "**C**" because this is the most appropriate place to break the paragraph into two separate sentences.

6. Sentence 1 provides key information concerning the purpose of the memo including the main event (e.g., the seizure of more than $60 million in counterfeit U.S. dollars) and the date this event took place. Sentence 7 provides an important segue from the first paragraph to the second, introducing new information that is a major focus of the second paragraph (e.g., partnerships with police forces in other countries). Sentence 9 provides key information that directly ties to the main purpose of the memo, but also provides unique and pertinent information. Additionally, Sentence 9

serves as an important preface to Sentence 10. Sentence 10 provides additional details about the topic at hand, and builds from Sentence 9, but does not speak directly about the specific event that is the focus of the memo. Thus, the correct response option is "**D**" because deleting Sentence 10 would have the least detrimental impact on the clarity of the memo, compared to the other sentences listed in the options provided. Though some information would be lost by deleting Sentence 10, the key purpose of the memo would still be present (in Sentence 1). Also, if Sentence 10 were deleted, the memo would still make logical sense in terms of the flow of ideas (this would be lost if Sentence 7 and/or Sentence 9 were deleted).

7. In Sentence 5, "french" should be capitalized to read "French." All other sentences listed as options use proper capitalization. Thus, the correct response option is "**B**."

8. In Sentence 10, "continue" should be "continues" because the subject for this verb (frequency) is singular. No other listed sentences contain subject-verb agreement errors. Thus, the correct response option is "**B**."

Passage 2:

U.S. Department of Homeland Security

United States Secret Service

**FORGERY INVESTIGATION
SUMMARY REPORT**

(1)On January 4th, 2010, Agents were called to the Check-2-Cash store on 4752 Wentworth Street in Minneapolis, MN. (2)Agents Carrie Furstill and Geoffrey Jansen arrived at the store and we're told that someone attempted to use forged identification documits in order to cash a government-issued check for $2,343.60. (3)The Agents interviewed the teller involved, Markus Hermann, to document the incidents. (4)Earlier that day, the subject enters the store, walked up to the teller, and said he would like to cash a check. (5)The teller took the check from underneath the glass barricade and proceaded to ask for identification. (6)The subject than presented what appear to be a state-issued identification card. (7)When he inspected it, Mr. Hermann notes that the card was missing a watermark and determined it to be a forged Identification.

(8)Mr. Hermann intended to report this to the authorities, so he told the subject that hed need to approve the large cash amount with her manager. (9)This allowed him to go in to the office and call the police. (10)The subject seemed nervous when Mr. Hermann turned to walk into the back office, at which point he turned and ran from the store. (11)He left behind the check and the ID. (12)Agent Furstill and Jansen contacted the original recipient of the check and determined that the check was stolen from an apartment mailbox shared by all residents, indicating all units in the building we're effected. (13)The victim didn't provide any leads as to who may have broken into the mailbox, nor did any of the other residence. (14)Security cameras caught several image of the subject, but identification wasn't made. (15)The case is currently opened as the Secret Service awaits further reports of fraudulent attempts to cash any additional checks that may have been in any other mailboxes.

Passage 2 Questions:

1. Which of the following sentences contains <u>exactly one</u> error?
    a) Sentence 6
    b) Sentence 7
    c) Sentence 12
    d) Sentence 13

2. Which of the following sentences contains <u>exactly three</u> errors?
    a) Sentence 8
    b) Sentence 9
    c) Sentence 1
    d) None of the above

3. Which of the following sentences contains an error in apostrophe use?
    a) Sentence 12
    b) Sentence 13
    c) Sentence 14
    d) Both A and C

4. Which of the following sentences contains a misspelled word?
    a) Sentence 5
    b) Sentence 7
    c) Sentence 8
    d) Sentence 15

5. Which of the following sentences contains an improperly used word?
    a) Sentence 6
    b) Sentence 8
    c) Sentence 10
    d) Sentence 14

6. Which of the following sentences contains an error in capitalization?
    a) Sentence 2
    b) Sentence 3
    c) Sentence 7
    d) Sentence 8

7. Which of the following sentences contains both an error in apostrophe use and an improperly used word?
    a) Sentence 12
    b) Sentence 13
    c) Sentence 14
    d) Sentence 15

8. Which of the following sentences contains an error in pronoun use?
    a) Sentence 4
    b) Sentence 7
    c) Sentence 8
    d) Sentence 11

Passage 2 Explanations:

1. Sentence 6 contains two errors: "than" should be "then" and "appear" should be "appears." Sentence 7 contains two errors: "notes" is the wrong tense and should be "noted" and "Identification" should not be capitalized. Sentence 12 contains three errors: "Agent" should be plural, "we're" should we "were," and "effected" should be "affected." Sentence 13 contains exactly one error: "residence" should be "residents," as it refers to the people who live there, not the actual place. Thus, the correct response option is "**D**" because among the options listed, only Sentence 13 contains exactly one error.

2. Sentence 8 contains two errors: "hed" is missing an apostrophe, and "her" is the incorrect pronoun given that it has been established that Mr. Hermann is male. Sentence 9 contains one error: "in to" should not have a space and should be one word. Sentence 1 contains no errors. Thus, the correct response option is "**D**" because none of the listed options contain exactly three errors.

3. Sentence 12 contains an error in apostrophe use because "we're" should be "were." Sentences 13 and 14 do not contain any errors in apostrophe use. Thus, the correct answer is "**A**" because it is the only sentence listed where there is an error in apostrophe use.

4. Sentence 5 contains the misspelled word "proceaded" which should be spelled "proceeded." Sentence 7 does not contain a misspelled word; the errors are in verb tense and use of punctuation. Sentence 8 contains an apostrophe error, but no misspelled words. Sentence 15 contains an error in verb tense, but no misspelled words. Thus, the correct answer is "**A**" because Sentence 5 is the only option listed that contains a misspelled word.

5. The word "than" is improperly used in Sentence 6. This is considered an improperly used word because it should be "then" instead of "then." This is an improperly used word and is NOT considered a spelling error because, though "than" is a real word and is correctly spelled, it has a different meaning than the appropriate word "then." Sentence 8 contains a pronoun use error. Sentence 10 contains no errors. Sentence 14 contains an error where "image" should be the plural "images." Thus, the correct response option is "**A**" because Sentence 6 contains an improperly used word.

6. Sentence 2 contains an apostrophe error and a spelling error. Sentence 3 contains an error in use of plurals. Sentence 7 contains an error in capitalization because "Identification" should not be capitalized, as it is not a proper noun. Sentence 8 contains an apostrophe error and a pronoun error. Thus, the correct answer is "**C**" because Sentence 7 is the only option listed that contains an error in capitalization.

7. Sentence 12 contains an error in apostrophe use because "we're" should be "were." It contains an improperly used word because "effected" should be "affected." This is an improperly used word and is NOT considered a spelling error because, though

"effected" is a real word and is correctly spelled, it has a different meaning than the appropriate word "affected." Sentence 13 Sentence 13 contains an improperly used word ("residence" should be "residents") but no error in apostrophe use. Sentence 14 contains an error where "image" should be the plural "images." Sentence 15 contains an error in verb tense, but no misspelled words. Thus, the correct answer is "**A**."

8. Sentence 4 contains an error in verb tense. Sentence 7 contains an error in capitalization because "Identification" should not be capitalized, as it is not a proper noun. Sentence 8 contains a pronoun error because "her" is the incorrect pronoun given that it has been established that Mr. Hermann is male. Sentence 11 contains no errors. Thus, the correct answer is "**C**" because Sentence 8 is the only option listed that contains a pronoun error.

EXPERIENCE INVENTORY, PART 2

OVERVIEW

The Experience Inventory, Part 2 contains statements that describe different situations and opinions.

For example, you may see questions such as:

1. You frequently need extra time to complete your work.

2. You accept responsibility when you make a mistake.

3. You follow work instructions, even when you would rather do things differently.

You must choose the response option that best reflects the extent to which your past supervisors and/or teachers would agree that the statement describes you. This section of the test is only asking about your past experiences, so there is no way to study for these questions. Therefore, be as accurate as possible in your answer choices. **Section 4 contains 96 questions and you will have 30 minutes to complete this section.**

TEST DIRECTIONS

This section contains statements that describe different situations and opinions. Read each statement carefully. Then, choose the response option that best reflects the extent to which **your past supervisors and/or teachers would agree that the statement describes you**. Fill in the circle on your answer sheet that corresponds to your response choice. Be sure to mark one, and only one, answer for each question or statement.

Use the following response option guide to respond to these statements:

> Your past supervisors and/or teachers would:
> a) Strongly disagree
> b) Disagree
> c) Neither agree nor disagree
> d) Agree
> e) Strongly agree

Please respond as accurately and honestly as possible (some questions are designed to detect inaccurate self-descriptions). It is best to work at a fairly rapid pace, without spending too much time thinking about any one question or statement.

DETAIL OBSERVATION

OVERVIEW

In this section, you are presented with a series of photographs. These photographs depict images you may see on the job; for example, a rope line or a city street during a surveillance operation. Next, you will answer a series of questions unrelated to the photographs. Then, you will answer a series of questions about what appeared in the photographs, but you are not permitted to view the photograph while answering these questions. This section contains 3 photographs and 3 sets of accompanying questions.

Each picture has an accompanying description. The test administrator will read this description and then you will have 2 ½ minutes to view the photograph.

Below are some things to consider when you are looking at the photographs:

- People: Consider what the people look like in the picture, what they appear to be doing, and other details about their appearance.

- Objects: Observe what objects appear in the photograph and their position in the picture.

- Background: Observe the overall setting and background features in the photograph.

- Try to anticipate what you might need to remember from the photograph.

- Practice viewing the sample photographs on the following pages based on the timing requirements to become familiar with how long will have to view the photographs.

After the viewing period has ended, you will be asked to answer a series of unrelated questions. On the actual test, there will be five Language Usage questions directly following all photographs in the Detail Observation Section. For the purposes of this guide, only one set of sample Language Usage questions are provided after Photograph 1 to illustrate the types of questions that will be asked.

TEST DIRECTIONS

In this section, you will be presented with color photographs that depict scenarios that a Secret Service Special Agent may encounter or observe on the job. You will be given a set amount of time to view each photograph. Next, you will be asked a series of questions unrelated to the photograph. Then, you will be asked a series of questions about the photograph; however, you will not be permitted to view the photograph while answering these questions.

For each photograph, the test will progress as follows:
- You will be given 2½ minutes to view the photograph, after which time you will be told to stop.
- Then, you will be given 5 minutes to complete the series of questions unrelated to what you observed in the photograph. You will <u>not</u> be able to move on until after the 5 minute period has ended.
- You will then be given 6 minutes to answer questions about the photograph.

You will not be allowed to take notes during this section of the test. You must answer the questions about the photograph based only upon your memory of the details in the photograph.

You are not permitted to turn back to the photograph once the initial 2 ½ minute viewing period has ended.

Language Usage

This portion of Section 5 contains 5 sentences. Each sentence is divided into four sections by slashes (/). You are to determine how many sections, if any, contain an error. The errors may be errors in grammar, punctuation, capitalization, spelling, or the formation of plurals.

Because many experts disagree on the appropriate use of commas in a sentence, we are **not** testing for this type of error. Therefore, even if you believe that a comma should be present or omitted, **do not** count that as an error.

If none of the sections contain errors, fill in the circle on your answer sheet that corresponds to "0 sections." If one section contains an error, fill in the circle on your answer sheet that corresponds to "1 section," and so on.

    A = 0 sections   B = 1 section   C = 2 sections   D = 3 sections   E = 4 sections

You will have 5 minutes to complete this portion of Section 5.

Sample Photograph 1

Description:

Secret Service Special Agents often work on task forces with other agencies to investigate crimes or plan protective events. The following picture presents a view of a meeting conducted with various agencies to investigate a pattern of financial crimes.

Sample Language Usage Questions:

Response Options:
A = 0 sections   B = 1 section   C = 2 sections   D = 3 sections   E = 4 sections

1. This effort won't / be successful without / a partner ship with / you're department.

2. All agents / must report / to an / assigned location.

3. He opened the / cases file, / noted several inconsistency, / and made changes.

4. I am investigating / several womens' claims / that property was stolen / from their cars.

5. All agents' / are required to / follow this / policies and procedures.

Language Usage Explanations:

1. Part 1 and Part 2 contain no errors. Part 3 contains an error because it should be "partnership." Part 4 also contains an error because "you're" should be "your." Thus, the correct response option is "C" because 2 sections of the sentence contain errors.

    The correct version of this sentence is:
    This effort won't / be successful without / a **partnership** with / **your** department.

2. Parts 1, 2, 3, and 4 all contain no errors. Thus, the correct response option is "A" because 0 sections of the sentence contain errors.

    The correct version of this sentence is:
    All agents / must report / to an / assigned location.

3. Part 1 contains no errors. Part 2 contains an error because file is singular so "cases" should be the singular "case." It should be "case file" or "cases files" to be correct. Part 3 contains an error because "several" indicates more than one inconsistency, so it should be "inconsistencies." Part 4 contains no errors. Thus, the correct response option is "C" because 2 sections of the sentence contain errors.

    The correct version of this sentence is:
    He opened the / **case** file, / noted several **inconsistencies**, / and made changes.

4. Part 1 contains no errors. Part 2 contains an error because the plural possessive form of women is "women's." Part 3 and Part 4 contain no errors. Thus, the correct response option is "B" because 1 section of the sentence contains an error.

    The correct version of this sentence is:
    I am investigating / several **women's** claims / that property was stolen / from their cars.

5. Part 1 contains an error because "agents'" should not be possessive, so it should be "agents'." Part 2 contains no errors. Part 3 contains an error because it should be possessive and thus be "these." Part 4 contains no errors. Thus, the correct response option is "C" because 2 sections of the sentence contain errors.

    The correct version of this sentence is:
    All **agents** / are required to / follow **these** / policies and procedures.

Sample Photograph 1 Questions:

1. Which of the following objects was closest to the phone?
   a. a coffee mug
   b. a trash can
   c. a stack of paper clips
   d. a pencil

2. What color was the coffee mug on the table?
   a. black and green
   b. black and white
   c. blue and gold
   d. blue and red

3. Which of the following appeared in the picture?
   a. a blank flip chart
   b. an exit sign
   c. a blue notebook
   d. a woman in a black suit jacket

4. How many chairs were visible in the picture?
   a. five
   b. six
   c. seven
   d. eight

5. How many expanding file folders were stacked in the middle of the table?
   a. two
   b. three
   c. four
   d. five

6. What color was the suit jacket of the person sitting to the far right?
   a. blue
   b. black
   c. gray
   d. purple

7. Which of the following is NOT true about the women with gray hair in the photograph?
    a. She is wearing a gray suit jacket
    b. She is wearing glasses
    c. She is wearing a purple shirt
    d. She is holding a blue pen

8. What was the color of the tie worn by the man sitting on the far left of the photograph?
    a. green
    b. gold
    c. red
    d. blue

Photograph 1 Explanations:

1. The answer to the first question is "**D**" because among the objects listed, a pencil was closest to the phone. Other objects were closer or a similar distance to the phone (e.g., blue pens) but none of the objects were listed options.

2. The answer to the second question is "**C**" because the coffee mug on the table was blue with gold writing.

3. The answer to the third question is "**A**" because there is a blank flip chart in the background of the photograph. There is no exit sign, blue notebook, or a woman wearing a black suit jacket.

4. The answer to the fourth question is "**D**" because there were 8 chairs visible in the picture. Six of the chairs were around the table and two chairs were in the background of the photograph.

5. The answer to the fifth question is "**A**" because there are 2 expanding file folders stacked on the table: one brown folder and one red folder.

6. The answer to the sixth question is "**C**" because the woman sitting to the far right of the photograph is wearing a gray suit jacket.

7. The answer to the seventh question is "**B**" because the woman with gray hair is not wearing glasses. She is wearing a gray suit jacket, a purple shirt, and she is holding a blue pen.

8. The answer to the eighth question is "**C**" because the man is wearing a red tie.

Sample Photograph 2

Description:

Secret Service Special Agents investigate computer and financial crimes. During these investigations, Secret Service Special Agents may be asked to secure and canvass a crime scene in order to locate and preserve potential evidence. The following photograph presents a view of a counterfeiting crime scene that is part of a Secret Service Special Agent's investigation.

(Please note: No Language Usage sample questions will follow this sample photograph. Only questions related to the photograph will be presented.)

Photograph 2 Questions:

1. What color was the piece of paper on the paper cutter?
   a. green
   b. yellow
   c. white
   d. pink

2. How many pieces of paper were hanging from the bulletin board?
   a. five
   b. six
   c. seven
   d. eight

3. What was written on the open box sitting on the floor in front of the cabinets?
   a. Makes Your Work Look Better
   b. Makes Your Work Look Professional
   c. Makes Your Work Look Great
   d. Makes Your Work Look Pristine

4. There was a stack of paper on top of the island. This stack had paper of three colors including pink and what other two colors?
   a. yellow and blue
   b. green and yellow
   c. white and green
   d. blue and white

5. How many drawers were at least partially open?
   a. 2 of 8
   b. 2 of 10
   c. 3 of 8
   d. 3 of 10

6. How many tape dispensers appeared in the photograph?
   a. none
   b. one
   c. two
   d. three

7. Which of the following objects was closest to the canvas bag?
    a. a power cord
    b. manila envelopes
    c. a bulletin board
    d. a binder

8. Which of the following appeared in the photograph?
    a. a post-it note
    b. a telephone
    c. a red pen
    d. both (a) and (c)

Photograph 2 Explanations:

1. The answer to the first question is "**B**" because the piece of paper on the paper cutter was yellow.

2. The answer to the second question is "**D**" because there were 8 pieces of paper hanging from the bulletin board.

3. The answer to the third question is "**A**" because the writing on the box was "Makes your work look better."

4. The answer to the fourth question is "**C**" because the sheets of paper on top of the island were pink, white, and green.

5. The answer to the fifth question is "**A**" because there were 8 drawers, 2 of which were at least partially open in the photograph.

6. The answer to the sixth question is "**C**" because there were 2 tape dispensers that appeared in the photograph.

7. The answer to the seventh question is "**A**" because there was a power cord near the canvas bag that was closer than the manila envelopes, bulletin board, and binder.

8. The answer to the eighth question is "**D**" because both a post-it note and a red pen appeared in the photograph.

CHAPTER 3: SAEE TEST PREPARATION

This section provides tips for preparing for the SAEE, as well as test taking tips for the day of the test.

TEST PREPARATION TIPS

1. Review the directions and sample questions provided in this preparation guide so that you are familiar with the format and content of the test.

2. Practice going through each of the test sections to ensure you understand the directions and types of questions on the test before you take it.

3. Be sure to get enough sleep in the days leading up to the test.

4. Exercising in the days leading up to the test can help reduce stress.

5. Minimize stress on the test day by making sure you know how to get to the test location and how long it will take you. It is a good idea to make a "practice run" to the test location before the day of the test.

6. Plan to arrive at the test location early on the test day.

7. The night before the test, set an alarm and have a back-up alarm as well to ensure you arrive on time.

8. Eat a good breakfast on the morning of the test.

9. Wear a watch so that you can keep track of time for yourself as you take the test.

10. Remember to bring an acceptable form of photo ID to the test location.

TEST TAKING TIPS

1. Read all directions carefully. It will be helpful to familiarize yourself with the directions for each section prior to taking the test.

2. Read the entire question and all answer options before selecting a response. This will help ensure you understand what the question is asking and which answer choice is the best answer.

3. You will not be penalized for guessing. Therefore, it is to your advantage to answer each question. If you do not know the answer, try to eliminate one or two of the answer choices and make your best guess.

4. Do not spend too much time on any one question.

5. Check your answer sheet periodically to ensure that you are filling in your answer sheet correctly.

6. If you finish a section and have time remaining, go back and review your answers **within that section only.**

7. Try to stay calm and keep a positive attitude throughout the test. Do not panic if you do not know an answer. Take a deep breath and do your best with each question.

8. Do not worry about how fast someone else finishes his or her test. Focus on your own test.

9. Double-check your answers. Go back through the answer sheet (if time allows) to make sure the answers you intended to select are marked and reflect what you believe is the best answer to the question. This will help minimize mistakes due to carelessness.

10. Do not select responses based on the pattern of answers. Response options are randomly selected as the correct answer and do not follow any identifiable pattern.

11. Make sure to erase answers clearly if you change your response. This will help reduce errors in the scoring process.

CPSIA information can be obtained at www.ICGtesting.com
Printed in the USA
BVOW04s1318250615

406180BV00005B/9/P